This Unique Unicorn Journal
belongs to

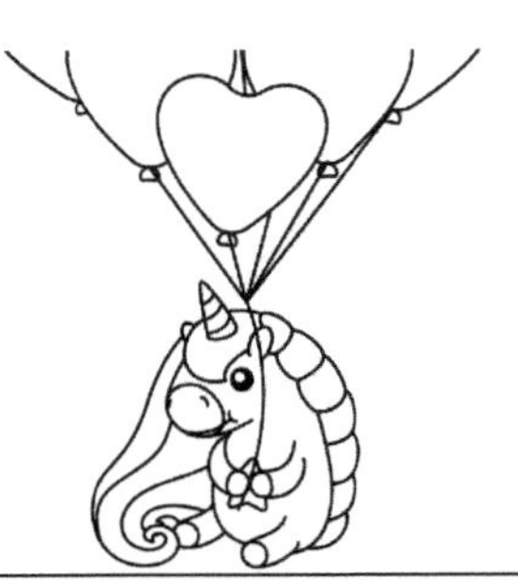

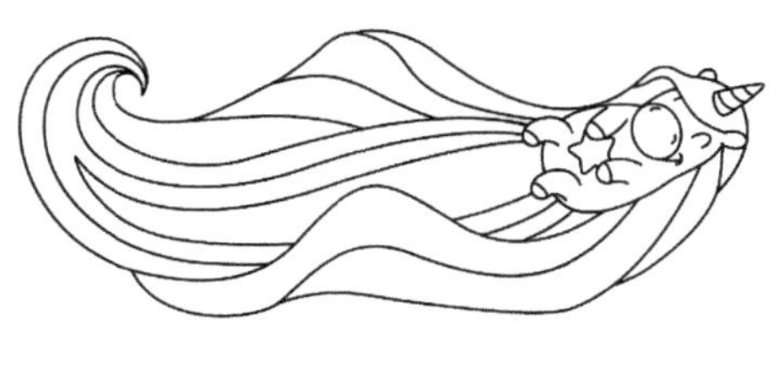

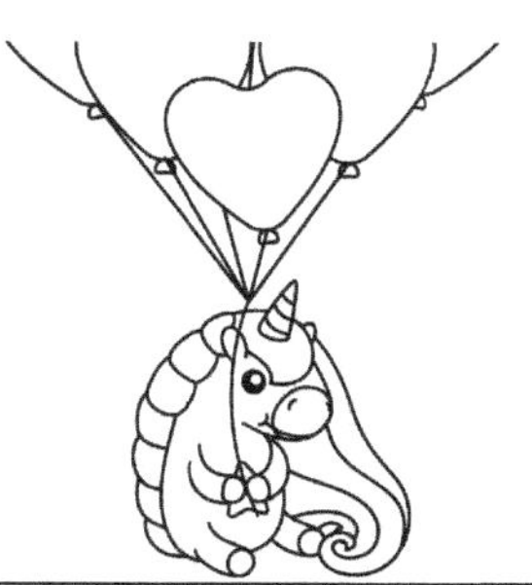

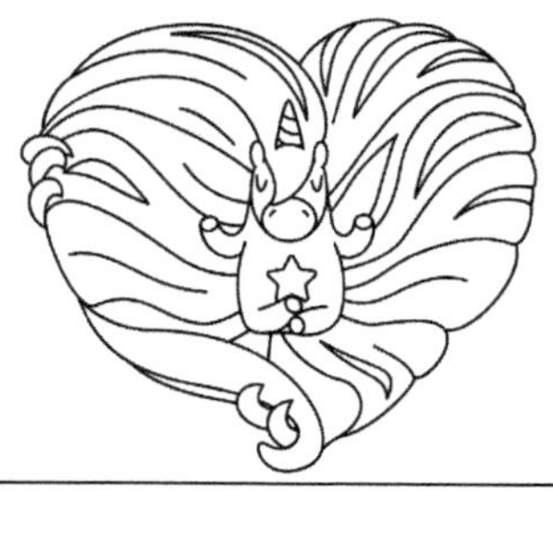

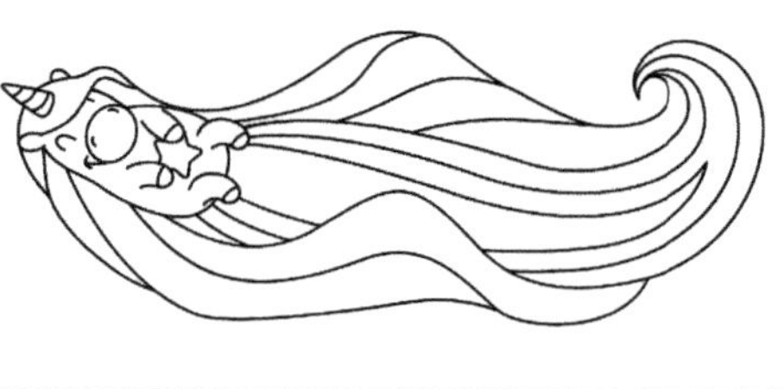

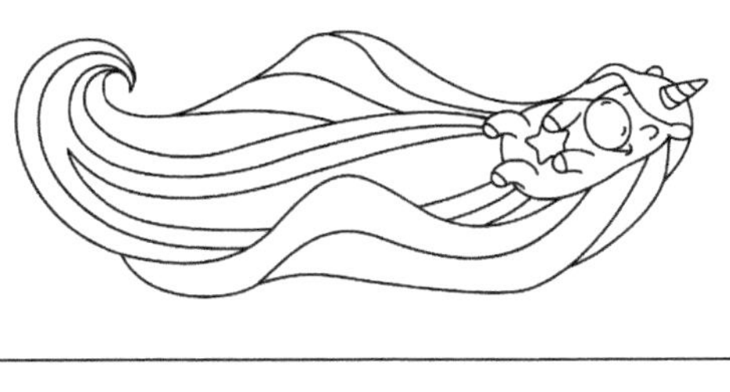

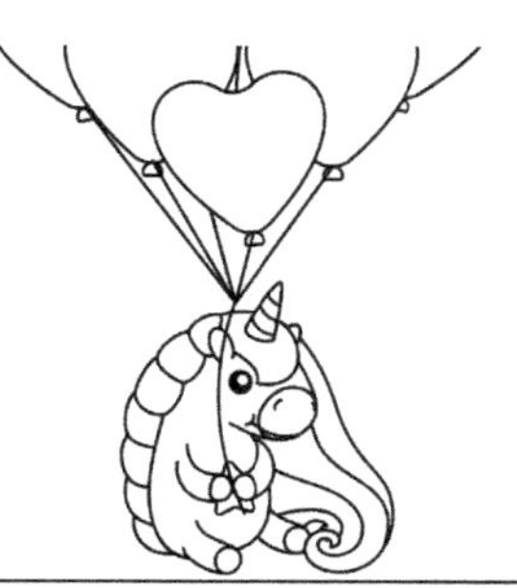

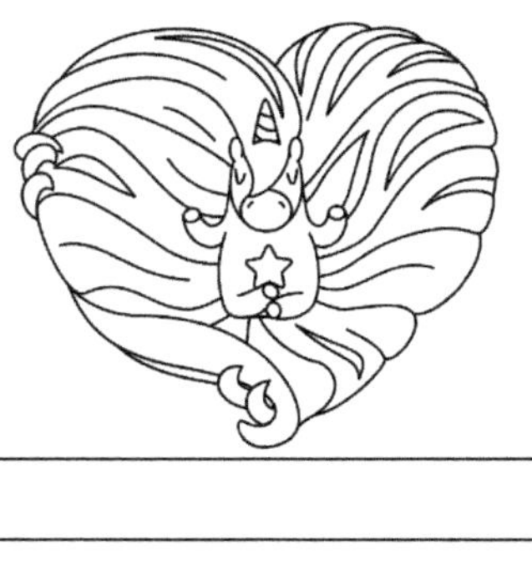

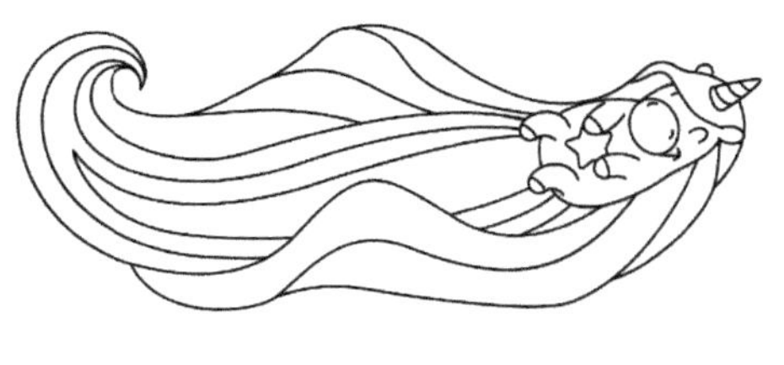

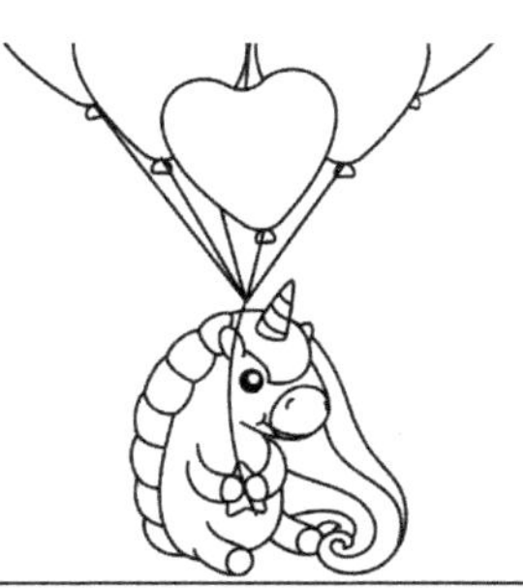

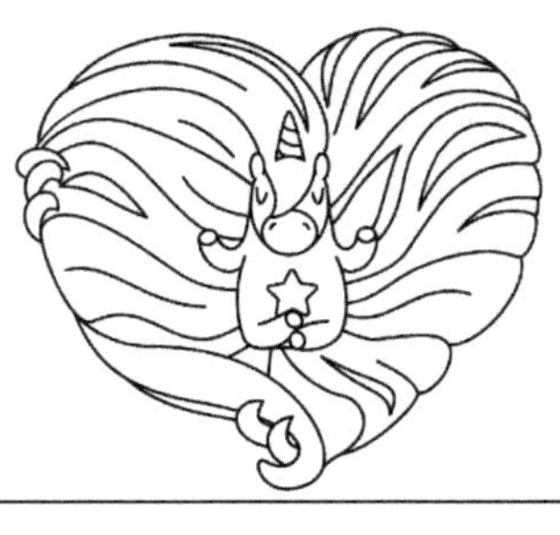

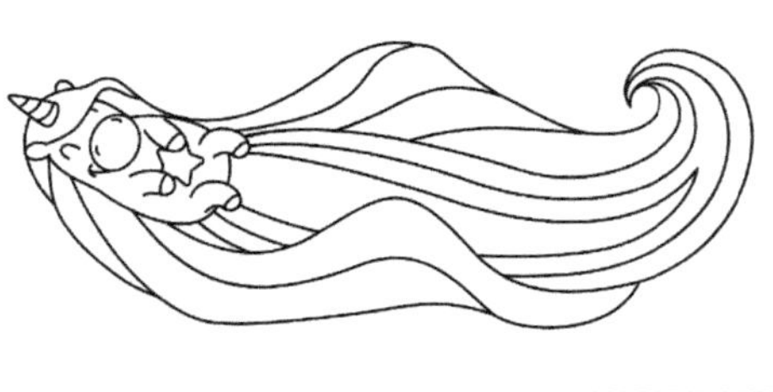

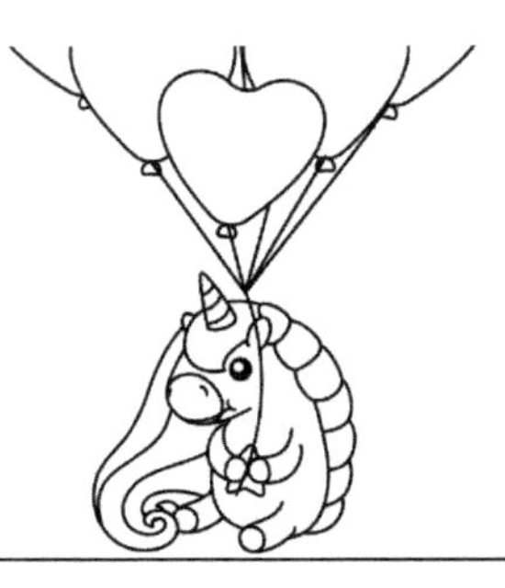

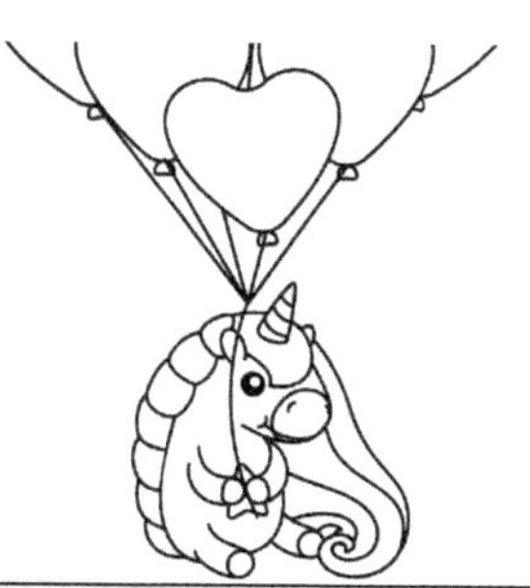

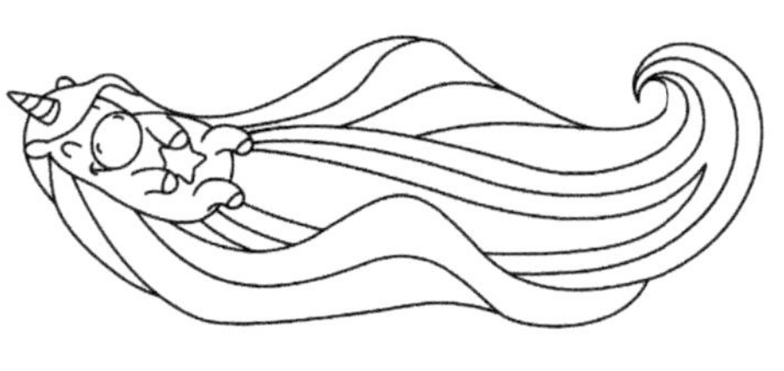

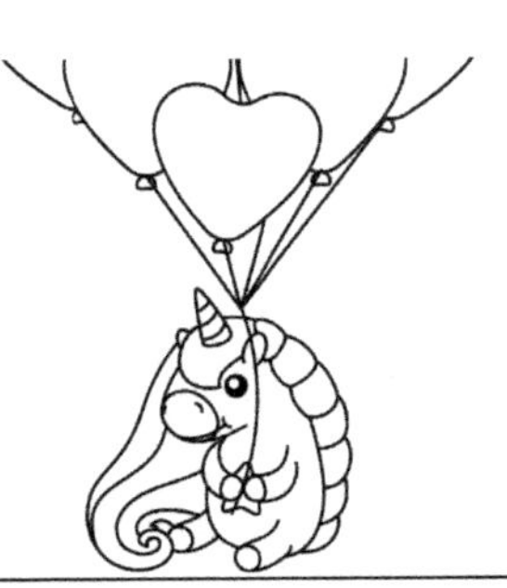

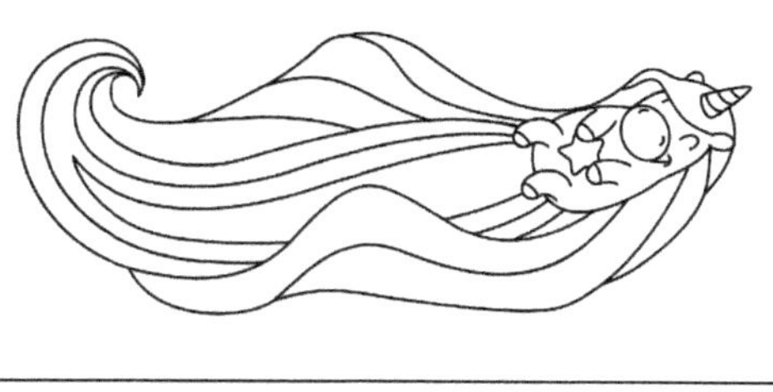

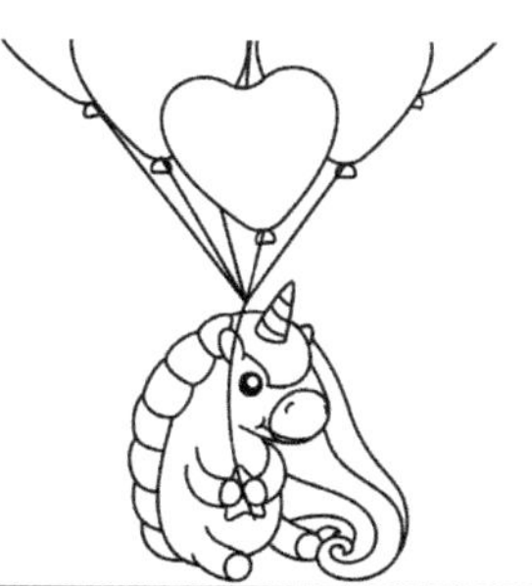

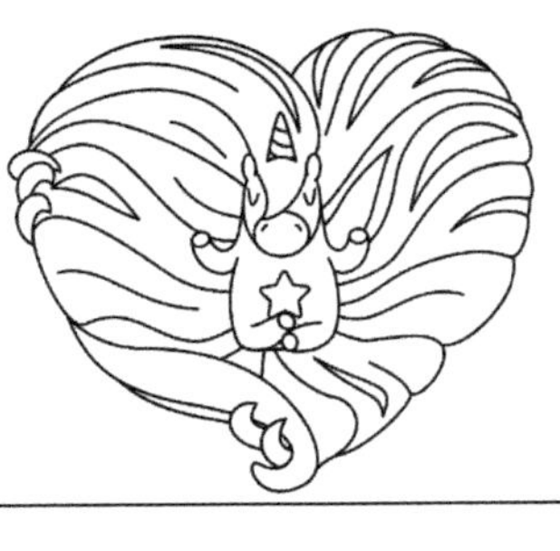

www.ingramcontent.com/pod-product-compliance
Lightning Source LLC
Chambersburg PA
CBHW051502050726

47593CB00005B/2181